THE ALMIGHTY BIBLE

A BIBLICALLY ACCURATE GRAPHIC NOVEL

2(4) This is the history of the generations of the heavens and of the earth...

Apple of the Eye Publishing
© 2010 Apple of the Eye

Available on iTunes for your iPhone and iPad
or visit us online at:

www.thealmightybible.com

Edited by Kevin O'Donnell
Illustration & Color by Malumworks
A Golden Dog Production
Book Design by Poets Road

Foreword

"In the beginning." So begins the book of Genesis, a story of beginnings. The opening chapters (1-11) tell the story of the origins of the universe and of human beings, indeed of everything that exists.

Genesis 1 and 2 picture a world of bliss. In Eden, human beings are in a harmonious relationship with God and thus with each other and all of creation.

In chapter 3, the plot of Genesis takes a downward turn as it recounts the first rebellion, the first murder, the first city, the origin of music, metal working, and languages. Genesis 3-11 tells stories of human sin and divine judgment. Even so, God stays involved with the creatures that he made, continually extending tokens of his grace to them.

A dramatic shift in the plot takes place in chapter 12. No longer is the focus of attention the whole world, but rather one person, Abraham. God's numerous judgments and acts of grace toward human beings have not brought them back into a harmonious relationship with him. They have continued to rebel. But now God seeks to restore the relationship with all human beings through a relationship with Abraham and Sarah and their descendants. If they obey him, then he will bless them. But more than that, he will bless "all the families of the earth" (12:3).

The story of Abraham and Sarah that makes up such a large part of the book of Genesis (12-25) is thus also a story of origins, in this case of the people of God, later known as Israel, through whom God intends to reach the world. Genesis chronicles Abraham's life as a journey of faith and fear as he reacts to various obstacles that threaten the promise that Abraham's descendants will become "a great nation" (12:2).

For Abraham's descendants to become "like the sand on the seashore" (22:17, 32:12), he and Sarah must have the first child, but she remains barren until late in life. Fearing that God will not come through, Abraham often tries to manufacture his own descendant leading to the birth of Isaac through a secondary wife Hagar.

But God's plan was for the true heir, Isaac, to be born well after the time when normal childbearing takes place. That way no one can miss the fact that this child was a gift from God. Many people today find their own struggles with faith mirrored in Abraham's life story (Heb. 11:8-12, 17-19).

The next chapters of Genesis continue the story of the so-called patriarchs, or fathers, of God's people Israel, namely Isaac and Jacob. It is also a story of matriarchs, or mothers, as well, since Rebekah and Sarah (and Leah) play obvious pivotal roles in the passing down of the divine promises from generation to generation.

The connection to the story of Israel and the following books of the Old Testament is obvious when God changes Jacob's name to Israel and his twelve sons bear the names of later tribes of the nation of Israel.

The story of Joseph ends the book of Genesis. The story is told with such fluidity and coherence that these chapters are often considered one of the earliest short stories ever written.

Joseph himself states the theme of the account of his life in chapters 37-50. In 50:20, he says to his brothers, "Even though you intended to harm me, God intended it for good, in order to preserve a numerous people, as he is doing today."

The brothers wanted to hurt him, Potiphar's wife wanted him to go to jail. The chief cupbearer forgot all about Joseph when he left prison. Joseph experienced one hardship after another.

But God used all of these things in order to bring Joseph to the side of Pharaoh, so he could create the conditions that would allow his family, the people of promise, to survive a horrible famine.

Genesis is indeed a book of beginnings. It is the foundation of the story of the exodus and the origins of Israel narrated in the books of Exodus through Deuteronomy. But really it is the foundation of the entire Bible, the introduction to both Old Testament (Hebrew Bible) and New Testament. The New Testament understands that the promises given to Abraham are ultimately fulfilled in Jesus Christ and those who enter into a relationship with him (Gal. 3:15-16).

Even apart from the foundational role it plays in the Scriptures shared by Judaism and Christianity, it is a wonderful story for all people, believers and unbelievers alike. From creation to Joseph, the book contains stories that amaze and entertain. The book is not only full of information that feeds the brain, but its stories stir our emotions and stimulate our imagination.

For this reason, the book of Genesis lends itself to the graphic novel format. When the book was first written, very few people actually read it. They heard it read to them and they pondered what they heard in their minds and hearts. With the invention of the printing press, more people read it, but still many people learned about Genesis through the artistic depiction of its stories in the beautiful stained glass windows of cathedrals.

"The Almighty Bible: Genesis" weds visual depiction with the words of the book in a way that will capture the imagination of all readers, religious and non-religious alike. The whole team has done a magnificent job of capturing the spirit of the book in a way that supports the powerful words of Genesis. So, settle back, open up your mind and imagination to an ancient book that still has tremendous contemporary impact.

Tremper Longman III, PhD
Robert H. Gundry Professor of Biblical Studies
Westmont College
Author of "How to Read Genesis" and over twenty other books

Acknowledgements

Our goal with The Almighty Bible is to tell these incredible stories with the deepst respect and reverence for them. There are many people involved in this quest. I'd like to thank a number of people for their great assistance in creating Genesis...

First of all, great thanks to Daniel Youngmok Park and the entire Apple of the Eye team, including his partner Maria Jung. They are tremendous partners who founded their company on true Christian principles which they reinforce every day with their actions.

Dr. H. Joon Lee has contributed his insight into this project and helps make it palatable to the business world. Dong H. Chung is the one who brought everyone together with his tireless trips back and forth to Korea. Booyoung Kim is the amazing director who has worked, with David Lee, around the clock creating the wonderful images you see. His whole team deserves great thanks, including Anderson Choi who has been a good friend through the years.

Professor Tremper Longman has graciously lent us his endless storehouse of knowledge and insight on this project.

We owe great thanks to the people who created the World English Bible, which itself is derived from the 1904 American Standard version. We have edited and rephrased some of their text into the most exciting and accurate linear story we could imagine. We have left the chapter and verse designations at the end of each page so you can always refer to your favorite bible for the full text – or get The Almighty Bible on the iPAD or iPhone where the full text is only a tap away!

God Bless,

Kevin O'Donnell

EDITOR
www.thealmightybible.com
July, 2010

GENESIS

GENESIS

n the beginning God created the heavens and the earth. God's Spirit was hovering over the surface of the waters. God said, "Let there be light," and here was light. God saw that it was good. (1:1–1:18)

God said, "Let the waters swarm with swarms of living creatures, and let birds fly above the earth." God created the large sea creatures. God blessed them, saying, "Be fruitful, and multiply." (1:20–1:22)

God said, "Let us make man in our image and have dominion over all the earth." Yahweh God formed man from the dust of the ground and breathed into his nostrils the breath of life, and man became a living soul. (1:25–1:27)

Yahweh God planted a garden in Eden and there he put the man. God commanded the man, saying, "Of every tree of the garden you may freely eat, but of the tree of the knowledge of good and evil, you shall not eat of it. For in the day that you eat of it, you will surely die." (2:8–2:15)

Yahweh God caused a deep sleep to fall on the man and he took one of his ribs. He made the rib into a woman. Therefore a man will join with his wife, and they will be one flesh. They were both naked, the man and his wife, and were not ashamed. (2:21–2:25)

Now the serpent was more subtle than any other animal, and he said to the woman, "Has God really said, 'You shall not eat of the tree in the center?' You won't die, for God knows that in the day you eat it, your eyes will be opened, and you will be like God, knowing good and evil." (3:1–3:5)

She took of its fruit and ate, and she gave some to her husband and he ate. The eyes of both of them were opened, and they knew that they were naked. They sewed fig leaves together and made themselves clothes. (3:6–3:7)

Yahweh called to the man, "Where are you?" The man said, "I heard your voice and I was afraid because I was naked, and I hid myself." God said, "Who told you that you were naked? Have you eaten from the tree that I commanded you not to eat from?" The woman said, "The serpent deceived me, and I ate." (3:9–3:11)

God said to the serpent "On your belly you shall go. I will put enmity between you and the woman. Her offspring will bruise your head and you will bruise his heel." To Adam he said, "Because you have eaten of the tree, you are dust and to dust you shall return." So he drove out the man and he placed the flame of a sword, which turned every way, to guard the way to the tree of life. (3:14–3:24)

The man knew Eve. She conceived and gave birth to Cain and again to Cain's brother Abel. As time passed, God respected Abel, but he didn't respect Cain, and Cain was very angry. Cain said to Abel, his brother, "Let's go into the field." And Cain killed him. (4:1–4:8)

God said to Cain, "Where is Abel?" He said, "I don't know. Am I my brother's keeper?" God said, "The voice of your brother's blood cries to me from the ground. Now you are cursed." Cain went out from God's presenceand lived in the land of Nod, east of Eden. (4:9–4:15)

This is the book of the generations of Adam.

Adam became the father of Seth.
Seth became the father of Enosh.
Enosh became the father of Kenan.
Kenan became the father of Mahalalel.
Mahalalel became the father of Jared.
Jared became the father of Enoch after
  he became the father of Methuselah.
Enoch walked with God. God took him.
Methuselah became the father of Lamech.
Lamech became the father of Noah.

Noah was five hundred years old, and Noah became the father of Shem. (5:1–5:32)

The Nephilim were in the earth in those days, and also after that, when God's sons came in to men's daughters. They bore children to them. Those were the mighty men who were of old, men of renown. God saw the wickedness of man, and God said, "I will destroy man." (6:4–6:7)

But Noah found favor in God's eyes. Noah walked with God. God said to Noah, "Make a ship of gopher wood. I bring the flood. Everything will die. But I will establish my covenant with you. Of every living thing you shall bring two into the ship." Thus Noah did. (6:8–6:22)

Noah was six hundred years old when the flood of waters came on the earth. The flood was forty days on the earth. The waters increased and lifted up the ship. All the high mountains were covered. Only Noah was left and those who were with him in the ship. (7:6–7:23)

After one hundred fifty days, the waters decreased. The ship rested on Ararat's mountains. Noah sent out a dove, but the dove found no place to rest, and she returned to him. Again he sent the dove out. The dove came back, and behold, in her mouth, was an olive leaf. So Noah knew that the waters were abated. (8:3–8:11)

God blessed Noah and his sons and said, "I have given everything to you. Be fruitful and multiply." God said, "This is the token of the covenant which I make between me and you. I set my rainbow in the cloud. I will look at it, that I may remember the everlasting covenant between God and every living creature." (9:1–9:15)

The whole earth was of one language. They said one to another, "Let's build a tower whose top reaches to the sky." God said, "Come, let's go down, and confuse their language, that they may not understand one another." So they stopped building the city called Babel. From there, God scattered them across the surface of all the earth. (11:1–11:8)

This is the history of the generations of Shem.

Shem became the father of Arpachshad two years after the flood. Arpachshad became the father of Shelah.

lah became the father of Eber.

r became the father of Peleg.

eg became the father of Reu.

u became the father of Serug.

rug became the father of Nahor.

ahor became the father of Terah.

Terah became the father of Abram. (11:10–11:25)

Now God said to Abram, "Get out of your country and from your relatives, and from your father's house, to the land that I will show you. I will make of you a great nation. I will bless those who bless you, and I will curse him who curses you. All of the families of the earth will be blessed in you." (12:1–12:3)

Abram took Sarai, his wife; Lot, his brother's son; all their substance and souls, and they went to the land of the Canaanite, Canaan. God appeared to Abram and said, "I will give this land to your seed." Abram built an altar there to God. He left from there to the mountain on the east of Bethel, and pitched his tent. There he built an altar and called on Yahweh. Abram traveled on toward the South. (12:5–12:9)

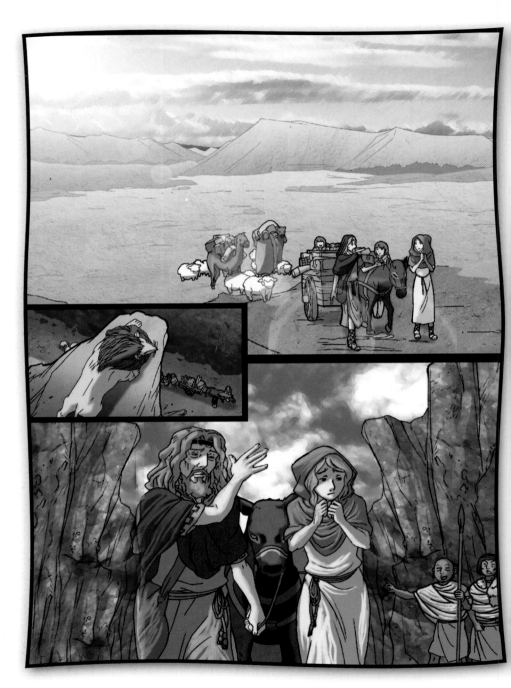

Abram traveled. There was a famine in the land. Abram went down into Egypt to live. He said to Sarai his wife, "You are a beautiful woman. When the Egyptians see you, they will kill me. Please say that you are my sister, that my soul may live because of you." (12:9–12:13)

When Abram reached Egypt, the Egyptians saw that Sarai was very beautiful. She was taken into Pharaoh's house. He dealt well with Abram for her sake: sheep, cattle, donkeys, servants, and camels. God plagued Pharaoh and his house because of Sarai, Abram's wife. (12:14–12:17)

Pharaoh called Abram and said, "What is this that you have done? Why didn't you tell me that she was your wife? Why did you say, 'She is my sister,' so that I took her to be my wife? Now take her, and go away." (12:17–12:19)

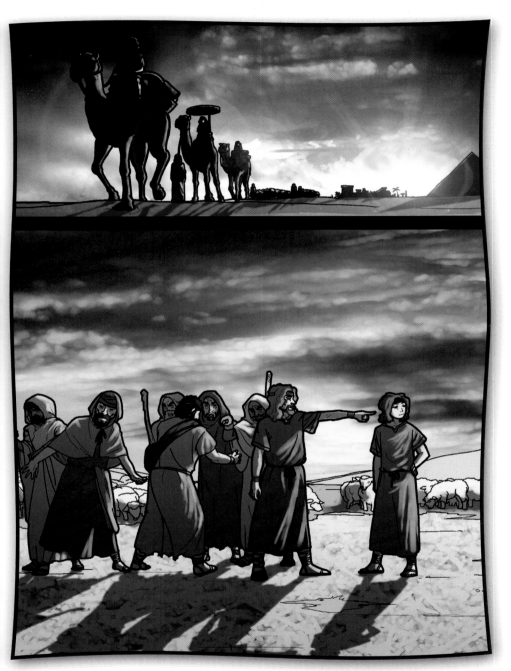

Abram was very rich in livestock, silver, and gold. He went to the place where his tent had been, to the place of the altar. There was strife between the herdsmen of Abram and the herdsmen of Lot. Abram said to Lot, "Please, if you go to the left then I will go to the right. Or if you go to the right hand, then I will go to the left." (13:1–13:9)

So Abram lived in Canaan, and Lot moved his tent to Sodom. Now the men of Sodom were exceedingly wicked and sinners against Yahweh. Yahweh said to Abram, "Now, look northward and southward and eastward and westward; for all the land which you see, I will give to you and to your offspring forever." (13:11–13:15)

The king of Sodom and the king of Gomorrah went to battle against Chedorlaomer, king of Elam; Tidal, king of Goiim; Amraphel, king of Shinar; and Arioch, king of Ellasar. The valley of Siddim was full of tar pits, and the kings of Sodom and Gomorrah fell there, and the victors took the riches. They took Lot and his possessions. (14:1–14:12)

When Abram heard that his relative was taken captive, he led out his three hundred eighteen trained men and followed them to Dan. He divided himself against them by night and struck them. He brought back all the goods, and also brought back Lot and his goods and people. (14:13–14:16)

Melchizedek, king of Salem, brought out bread and wine and said, "Blessed be Abram of God Most High, possessor of heaven and earth, who has delivered your enemies into your hand." The king of Sodom said to Abram, "Give me the people, and take the goods." Abram said, "I will accept nothing from you except the men who went with me." (14:17–14:24)

Yahweh came to Abram saying, "Abram, I am your shield, your great reward." Abram said, "Lord Yahweh, what will you give me since I go childless." Yahweh said, "Look to the sky and count the stars. So shall your seed be. I am Yahweh who brought you out of Ur of the Chaldees to give you this land to inherit it." (15:1–15:7)

A deep but horrible sleep fell on Abram, and Yahweh said to him, "Your seed will live as foreigners in a land that is not theirs. They will afflict them four hundred years. I will judge that nation harshly. Afterward, your seed will come out with great wealth, but long before, you will be buried in a good old age." (15:12–15:15)

Now Sarai, Abram's wife, was old and barren. She said to Abram, "Please go in to my handmaid, Hagar. I will obtain children by her." He went in to Hagar, and she conceived. When she had conceived, she looked at Sarai with contempt. Sarai dealt harshly with her, and Hagar fled. (16:1–16:6)

An angel found Hagar in the wilderness. He said, "Hagar, where are you going?" She said, "I am fleeing from Sarai." The angel said, "Return, for you will bear a son, Ishmael. He will be like a wild donkey. His hand will be against every man, and every man's hand against him." Abram was eighty-six years old when Hagar bore Ishmael. (16:7–16:16)

When Abram was Sarah is ninety-nine years old, Yahweh appeared. Abram fe
on his face as God said, "Your name is now Abraham, for I will make nation
of you. Kings will come out of you. I will establish my covenant between me an
you and your seed after you. I will be their God. Every male among you sha
be circumcised as a token of the covenant between me and you." (17:1–17:11

God said, "Sarai's name will be Sarah. I will bless her, and she will give you a son and be a mother of nations." Abraham fell and laughed, "Sarah is ninety-nine years old!" God said, "You shall call his name Isaac. As for Ishmael, I have blessed him. I will make him a great nation. But my covenant I establish with Isaac." (17:15–17:21)

Yahweh appeared to him. "The cry of Sodom and Gomorrah is great, and their sins grievous. I will go see whether their deeds are as bad as the reports which have come to me." Yahweh said, "If I find fifty righteous men in Sodom, then I will spare it." Abraham said, "What if ten are found there?" He said, "I will not destroy it for the ten's sake." (18:1–18:32)

Two angels came to Sodom. Lot urged them into his house and made them a feast. But the men of Sodom surrounded his house. "Where are the men who came in to you this night? Bring them out to us, that we may have sex with them." Lot said, "Please don't do anything to these men, because they have come under my roof." (19:1–19:8)

They said, "Now we will deal worse with you than with them!" They pressed hard on Lot. But the angels struck the men with blindness. They said to Lot, "Your daughters, and whoever you have in the city, bring them out, for we will destroy this place." (19:9–19:13)

In the morning, the angels hurried Lot, "Get up! Take your wife and daughters. Run for your life! Don't look behind you, lest you be consumed!" Then Yahweh rained down sulfur and fire. But Lot's wife looked back, and she became a pillar of salt. Abraham looked that morning toward Sodom and Gomorrah and saw the smoke. (19:15–19:27)

Yahweh visited Sarah, and Sarah conceived and bore Abraham a son in his old age. Abraham called his son, Isaac. Abraham was one hundred years old. Sarah saw the son of Hagar, Ishmael, mocking Isaac. She said to Abraham, "Cast out this handmaid and her son! For he will not be heir with my son, Isaac." (21:1–21:10)

Abraham rose in the morning, took bread, and gave bread and a bottle of water to Hagar and her child and sent her away. She wandered in the wilderness of Beersheba. The water was spent, and she cast the child under one of the shrubs. She went and sat a good way off. For she said, "Don't let me see the death of my son." She wept. (21:14–21:17)

The angel called to Hagar, "Don't be afraid. For God has heard the voice of the boy." He opened her eyes, and she saw a well of water. She filled the bottle and gave the boy drink. God was with the boy, and he grew and became an archer. He lived in the wilderness of Paran. His mother took a wife for him out of the land of Egypt. (21:17–21:21)

It happened after these things that God tested Abraham. He said, "Take your son Isaac and offer him as a burnt offering." Abraham rose, saddled his donkey, and took Isaac. On the third day, Abraham took the wood of the burnt offering and laid it on Isaac his son. He took in his hand the fire and the knife. (22:1–22:4)

Isaac spoke. "Father? Here is the fire and the wood, but where is the lamb for a burnt offering?" Abraham said, "God will provide himself the lamb my son." Abraham stretched out his hand to kill his son. The angel of Yahweh called to him, "Abraham, Abraham! Don't lay your hand on the boy. For now I know that you fear God since you have not withheld your son from me." (22:7–22:12)

Abraham looked and saw a ram caught in the thicket and offered him up for a burnt offering instead of his son. The angel called to Abraham a second time and said, "Because you have not withheld your only son, I will bless you and multiply your seed greatly like the stars of the heavens. All the nations of the earth will be blessed because you have obeyed my voice." (22:13–22:18)

Sarah lived one hundred twenty-seven years. Then Abraham buried Sarah in a cave in the land of Canaan. Abraham said to his servant, "Please go to my country, and to my relatives, and find a wife for my son, Isaac. Yahweh will send his angel before you." The servant took ten camels, arose, and went to Nahor, in Mesopotamia. (23:1–24:10)

He made the camels kneel down outside the city by the well as women came to draw water. He said, "Yahweh, let it happen, that the young lady to whom I will say, 'Please let down your pitcher that I may drink,' will say, 'Drink, and I will also give your camels a drink,' and let her be the one you have appointed for Isaac." (24:11–24:14)

Rebekah came with her pitcher. She was very beautiful. The servant ran to her and said, "Please give me a drink from your pitcher." She said, "Drink, my lord." She gave him drink and then said, "I will also draw for your camels." She emptied her pitcher into the trough and ran again to the well for all his camels. (24:14–24:20)

The man took a golden ring and two bracelets and said, "Whose daughter are you?" She said to him, "I am the daughter of Bethuel, the son of Milcah." He said, "Blessed be Yahweh who has led me to the house of my master's relatives." (24:21–24:27)

The man came into her house and said, "The God of my master Abraham led me here to take my master's brother's daughter for his son." Then Laban, Rebekah's brother, answered, "Take her and go, as Yahweh has spoken." The servant gave jewels to Rebekah and precious things to Laban and her mother. Rebekah arose with her ladies and followed the man on camels. (24:32–24:61)

Isaac went out to meditate in the field in the evening. He lifted up his eyes, and behold, there were camels coming. Rebekah lifted up her eyes, and when she saw Isaac, she took her veil and covered herself. Isaac brought her into his mother Sarah's old tent. (24:63–24:67)

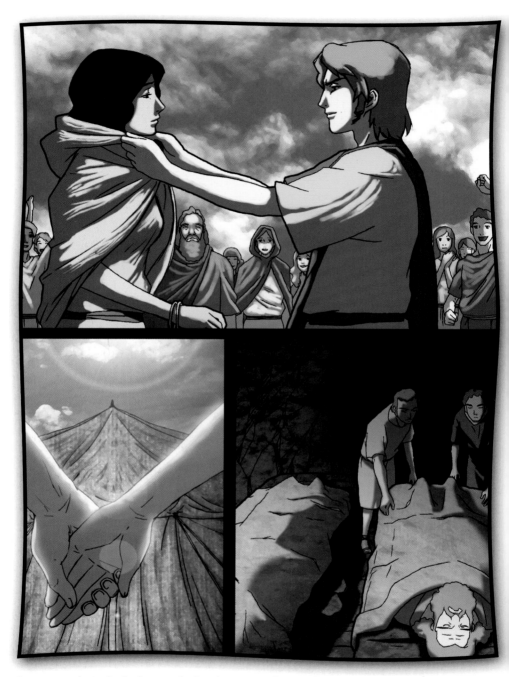

Isaac took Rebekah, and she became his wife. He loved her. Isaac was comforted after his mother's death. Abraham died in a good old age. Isaac and Ishmael buried him in the cave next to Sarah. (24:67–25:9)

Isaac prayed because Rebekah was barren, and she soon became pregnant. Yahweh said to her, "Two nations are in your womb. The elder will serve the younger." The first, Esau, came out red all over, with his brother, Jacob, holding onto his heel. The boys grew. Esau, who Isaac loved, was a skillful hunter. Jacob, who Rebekah loved, was a quiet man. (25:20–25:28)

There was a famine in the land. Yahweh appeared to Isaac and said, "Don't go down into Egypt. Live in this land, and I will be with you and will bless you because Abraham obeyed my voice and my commandments." Issac did as God commanded, and he grew great. The Philistines envied him. (26:1–26:14)

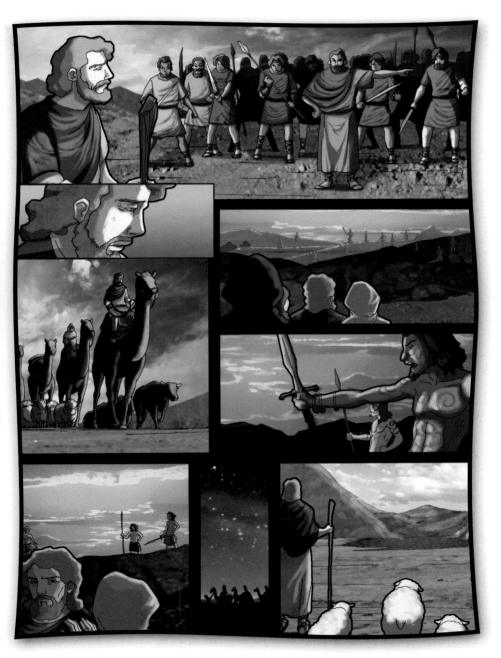

Isaac reaped one one hundred times what he planted that year. Abimelech said to Isaac, "Go from us." Isaac went to the valley of Gerar, and his servants dug a well. The herdsmen of Gerar argued with Isaac's herdsmen, saying, "The water is ours." Isaac and his people left that place and dug another well. He gave thanks, saying, "Yahweh has made room for us, and we will be fruitful here." (26:12–26:22)

He went from there to Beersheba where Yahweh appeared to him and said, "I am the God of Abraham your father. Don't be afraid, for I am with you and will bless you and multiply your seed for my servant Abraham's sake." Isaac built an altar there, and his servants dug a well. (26:23–26:25)

It happened that when Isaac was old and his eyes dim, he called Esau and said to him, "I am old and my death approaches. Take your quiver and your bow out to the field and take me venison. Make me savory food, such as I love, and bring it to me, that I may eat, and that my soul may bless you before I die." (27:1–27:4)

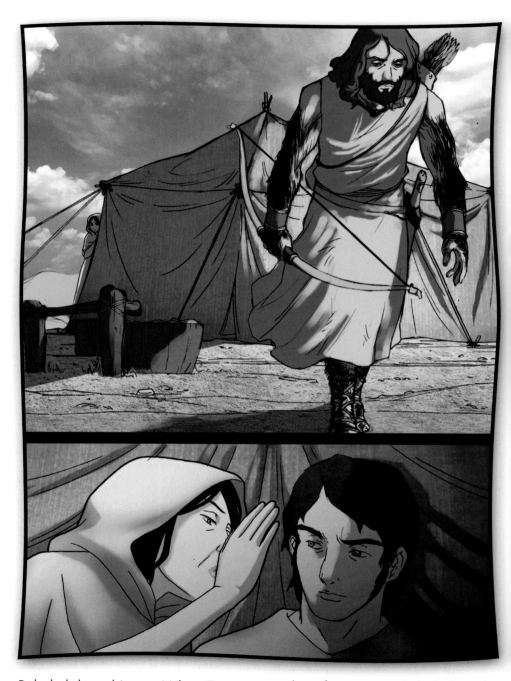

Rebekah heard Isaac. When Esau went to hunt for venison, Rebekah spoke to Jacob, "Now my son, obey my voice. Go get me two good young goats. I will make them savory food for your father, such as he loves. You shall bring it to your father, that he may eat and bless you before his death." (27:5–27:10)

Jacob said to Rebekah, "Esau is a hairy man. What if my father touches me? I will seem to him a deceiver, and I would bring a curse on myself and not a blessing." His mother said to him, "Let your curse be on me, my son. Only obey my voice, and go get them for me." (27:11–27:13)

Jacob brought them to his mother. His mother made savory food and took the good clothes of Esau and put them on Jacob. She put the skins of the young goats on his hands and on the smooth of his neck. She gave the savory food to Jacob. (27:14–27:17)

Jacob came to his father and said, "My father? I am Esau your firstborn. Please eat of my venison, that your soul may bless me." Isaac said, "How is it that you have found it so quickly?" He said, "Because God gave me success." Isaac said, "Please come near, that I may feel you, my son, whether you are really Esau or not." (27:18–27:21)

Isaac felt him and said, "The voice is Jacob's voice, but the hands are the hands of Esau. Are you really my son Esau?" Jacob said, "I am." Isaac ate and he drank, then said, "Come near now and kiss me, my son." Jacob came near and kissed him. Isaac smelled the smell of his clothing and blessed him. (27:22–27:27)

"God give you of the dew of the sky, of the fatness of the earth, and plenty of grain and new wine. Let peoples serve you and nations bow down to you. Be lord over your brothers. Let your mother's sons bow down to you. Cursed be everyone who curses you. Blessed be everyone who blesses you." (27:28–27:29)

It happened, as soon as Isaac had finished blessing Jacob, that Esau came in from his hunting. He said to his father, "Let my father arise and eat of his son's venison, that your soul may bless me." Isaac said to him, "Who are you?" He said, "I am your son, your firstborn, Esau." (27:30–27:32)

Isaac trembled and Esau cried, "Bless me, also, my father." Isaac answered, "Behold, I have made Jacob your lord. With grain and new wine have I sustained him." Esau wept as Isaac gave him a lesser blessing, "By your sword will you live, and you will serve your brother. It will happen, when you will break loose, that you shall shake his yoke from off your neck." (27:33–27:40)

Esau said, "The days of mourning for my father are at hand. Then I will kill my brother Jacob." The words of Esau were told to Rebekah. She sent and called Jacob, "Arise, flee to Laban, my brother, in Haran." (27:41–27:43)

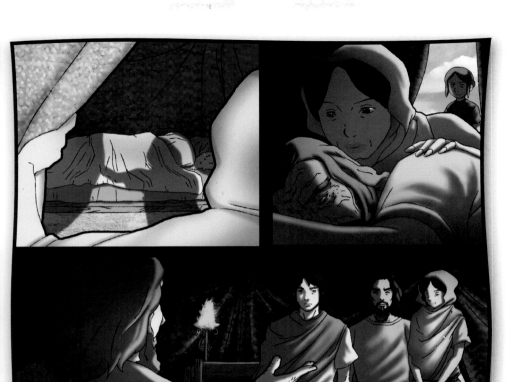

Rebekah slyly said to Isaac, "If Jacob takes a wife from the women here, what good will my life do me?" Isaac called Jacob, "You shall not marry one of the daughters of Canaan. Take a wife from the daughters of Laban." Esau went and took Mahalath, the daughter of Ishmael, to be his wife. (27:46–28:9)

Jacob went out from Beersheba and went toward Haran. That night, he dreamed of a stairway reaching from earth to heaven with the angels of God ascending and descending on it. Yahweh stood above it and said, "I am with you and will keep you, wherever you go and will bring you again into this land." (28:10–28:15)

Jacob awakened, afraid, "This is the gate of heaven." Early in the morning, he took the stone that he had put under his head, set it up for a pillar, and poured oil on it. He called that place Bethel. Jacob vowed, "If God will be with me so that I come again to my father's house in peace, Yahweh will be my God, and of all that you give me, I will give one tenth to you." Then Jacob went on his way. (28:16–29:1)

Jacob looked and saw a well in the field with a large stone covering it. Shepherds rolled the stone away and watered the sheep then put the stone back in its place. Jacob said to them, "Do you know Laban, the son of Nahor?" They said, "We know him. See, Rachel, his daughter, is coming with the sheep." (29:2–29:5)

Rachel came with her father's sheep. Jacob rolled the stone from the well's mouth and watered the flock of Laban. Jacob kissed Rachel and wept. Jacob told Rachel that he was her father's sister's son. Rachel ran and told her father. (29:9–29:12)

When Laban heard the news, he ran to meet Jacob and embraced him and brought him to his tent. Laban said to Jacob, "Because you are my brother, tell me, what will your wages be?" Jacob loved Rachel. He said, "I will serve you seven years for Rachel, your younger daughter." (29:13–29:18)

Jacob served seven years for Rachel. They seemed to him but a few days, because of the love he had for her. Jacob said to Laban, "Give me my wife, for my days are fulfilled." Laban made a feast. Then he took Leah, his daughter, and brought her to Jacob, who was drunk with wine. (29:20–29:23)

In the morning, Jacob saw it was Leah, and he said to Laban, "Didn't I serve with you for Rachel? Why have you deceived me?" Laban said, "It is not done to give the younger before the firstborn. I will give you Rachel, also, for yet seven more years of service." Jacob agreed and then he went in to Rachel, who he loved much more than Leah. (29:25–29:30)

It was Leah, however, who bore Jacob a son, Reuben. She bore another son and said, "Because Yahweh knows I am hated, he has given me this son, also." She conceived again and again. Rachel envied her sister and said to Jacob, "Give me children or else I will die." Jacob was angry, "Am I in God's place, who has withheld from you the fruit of the womb?" (29:32–30:2)

Rachel said, "Go in to my maid Bilhah that she may bear on my knees and I may obtain children by her." Jacob went in to Bilhah, who soon bore him a son. Rachel said, "God has heard my voice and has given me a son." Bilhah conceived again and bore Jacob a second son. Rachel said, "I wrestled with my sister and have prevailed." (30:3–30:8)

Leah took Zilpah, her handmaid, and gave her to Jacob as a wife. Then Leah herself bore Jacob a fifth son. Leah conceived again and bore a sixth son to Jacob. Afterwards, she bore a daughter and named her Dinah. God remembered Rachel, opened her womb, and she finally bore a child, who they named Joseph. (30:9–30:24)

After seven years, Jacob said to Laban, "Send me away to my own country." Laban said, "What can I give you so that you stay here, for Yahweh has blessed me because of you." Jacob said, "I will pass through your flock today removing every black sheep and spotted goat. This will be my hire." Laban agreed. (30:25–30:34)

Jacob took the herds three days' journey, and he set rods in the watering troughs whenever the stronger of the flock came to conceive. The rods produced black sheep and spotted goats. But when the flocks were feeble, he didn't put them in. So the feebler were Laban's and the stronger Jacob's. (30:36–30:42)

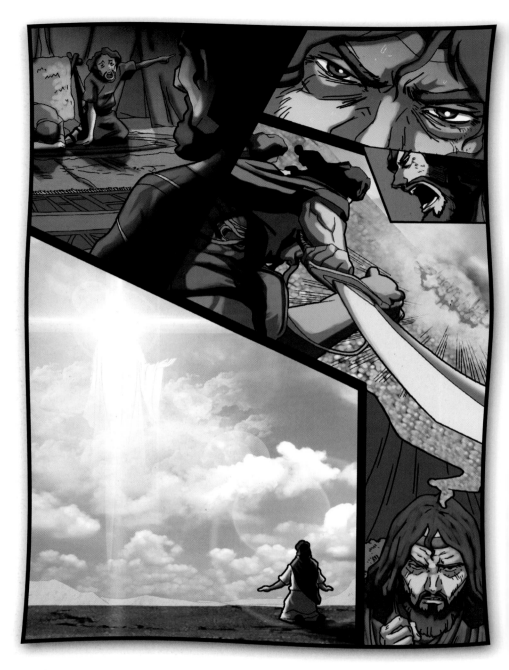

Jacob grew rich with large flocks, servants, camels, and donkeys. He heard the words of Laban's sons, "Jacob has taken away all that was our father's." Jacob saw that Laban was angry, and Yahweh said to Jacob, "Return to the land of your fathers and to your relatives and I will be with you." (30:43–31:3)

Jacob said to Rachel and Leah. "Your father has deceived me many times, but God has given his best livestock to me and told me to return home." They answered, "He has sold us and devoured our money. Do as God says." Jacob fled with all that was his, but first, Rachel stole idols from her father's tent. Laban was angry and pursued them. (31:4–31:22)

God came to Laban in a dream, "Don't speak to Jacob either good or bad."
Laban caught up with Jacob. "It is in the power of my hand to hurt you, but
the God of your father spoke to me last night. Now, you want to be gone,
but why have you stolen my gods?" Jacob answered, "Anyone you find your
gods with shall not live." Jacob didn't know that Rachel had stolen them.
(31:24–31:32)

Rachel had hidden the idols in a camel's saddle lying in her tent, which she sat upon. Laban looked throughout the tent, but when he came to Rachel, she said to her father, "Don't let my lord be angry that I can't rise up before you for I'm having my period." He searched but didn't find the idols and gave up. (31:34–31:35)

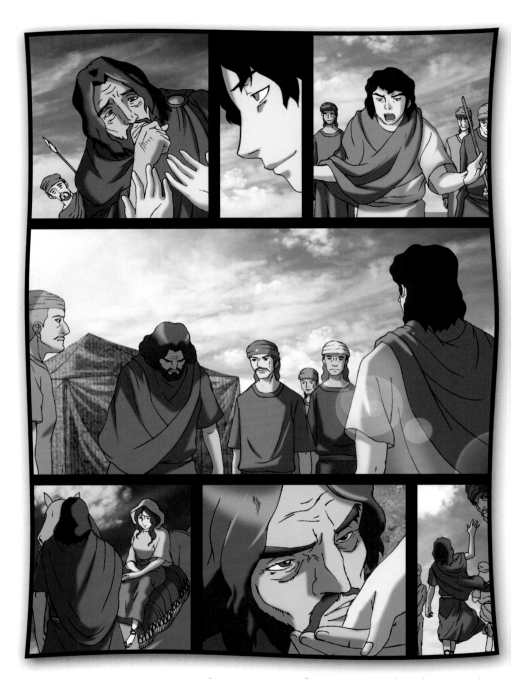

Jacob was angry. "I served fourteen years for your two daughters and six years for your flock, and you have changed my wages ten times. Unless the God of Abraham and the fear of Isaac had been with me, you would send me away empty. God has seen my affliction and rebuked you." Early in the morning, Laban rose up and departed. (31:36–31:55)

Jacob went on his way, and the angels of God met him. Jacob said, "This is God's army." Jacob sent messengers in front of him to Esau, his brother. The messengers returned, saying, "We found Esau and he comes to meet you with four hundred men." Then Jacob was greatly afraid and distressed. (32:1–32:7)

Jacob divided the people into two companies and said, "If Esau comes and attacks one company, then the other will escape." Jacob prayed, "God of Abraham and of my father, Isaac, who said to me, 'Return to your country, and I will do you good.' Please deliver me from the hand of my brother, for I fear he comes to strike me." (32:7–32:11)

Jacob took two hundred female goats and twenty male goats, two hundred ewes and twenty rams, thirty milk camels and their colts, forty cows and ten bulls, and twenty female donkeys, and ten foals and said to his servants, "When Esau meets you, say, 'These are your servant, Jacob's, who sends them as a present.'" For, Jacob said, "If I appease him with the present perhaps he will accept me." (32:13–32:18)

Jacob crossed the Jabbok River and wrestled with a man until morning. When the man saw that he couldn't prevail, he touched Jacob's thigh, and it was hurt. The man said, "Let me go." But Jacob said, "I won't let you go unless you bless me." He said, "Your name is no longer Jacob, but Israel, for you have fought with God and with men and have prevailed." (32:22–32:28)

As Esau's army approached, Jacob put the handmaids and their children in front, Leah and her children after, and Rachel and Joseph at the rear. He himself passed over in front of them and bowed himself to the ground seven times until his brother was upon him. (33:1–33:3)

But Esau ran to meet Jacob, kissed him, and they wept. He saw the women and the children. Esau said, "What do you mean by all the gifts you sent?" Jacob said, "To find favor in the sight of my lord." Esau said, "I have enough, my brother." But Jacob urged him, and Esau accepted the gift. (33:4–33:11)

Esau said, "Let us go." But Jacob said to him, "The children are tender, and the flocks and herds have their young, and if they overdrive them one day, they will die. Please, I will follow, gently, until I come to my lord at Seir." (33:12–33:14)

So Esau returned that day to Seir. Jacob came to the city of Shechem. Dinah, the daughter of Leah, went out to see the land. The son of the prince of the land, saw her. He took her, and his soul joined to hers, and he loved Dinah. Shechem spoke to his father, Hamor, saying, "Get me Dinah as a wife." (33:16–34:4)

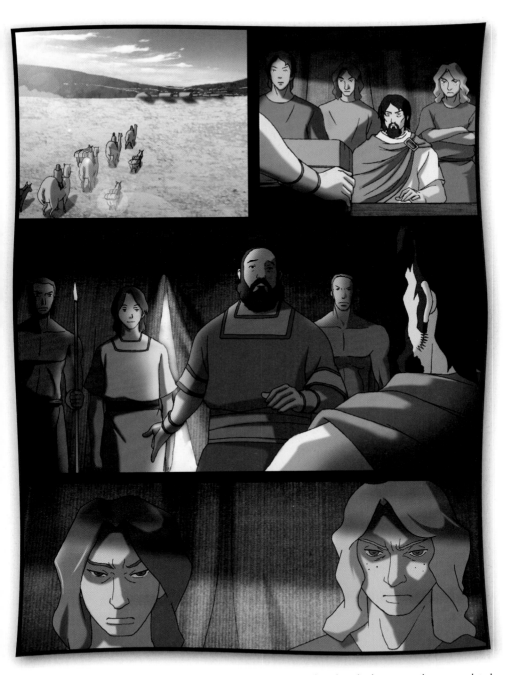

The sons of Jacob were very angry, because he had done a thing, which ought not to be done. Hamor talked with them, "The soul of my son, Shechem, longs for your daughter. Make marriages with us. Take our daughters for yourselves. You shall dwell with us." Shechem said, "I will give whatever you ask of me but give Dinah." (34:6–34:12)

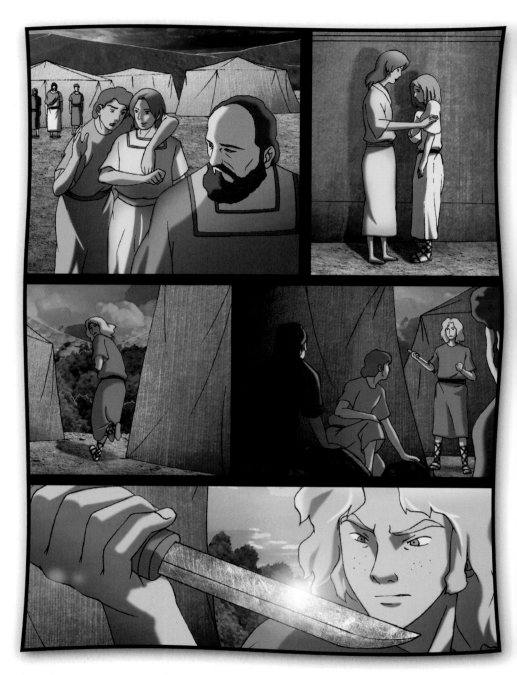

Jacob's sons answered with deceit, "If every male of you be circumcised, then will we give our daughters to you, and we will take your daughters to us, and we will dwell with you, and we will become one people. But if you will not be circumcised, then we will take our sister and be gone." (34:13–34:17)

Hamor and Shechem came to the gate of their city and talked with the men, "These men are peaceful. Let us take their daughters and give them ours." And every male was circumcised. On the third day, when they were sore, two of Dinah's brothers came and killed all the males. They took Dinah out of Shechem's house and went away. (34:20–34:26)

Jacob said to Simeon and Levi, "You make me odious to the others in this land. We are few in number. They will gather themselves together and we will be destroyed." God said to Jacob, "Arise, go up to Bethel, and live there." Then Jacob said to all who were with him, "Put away the foreign gods; purify yourselves." (34:30–35:3)

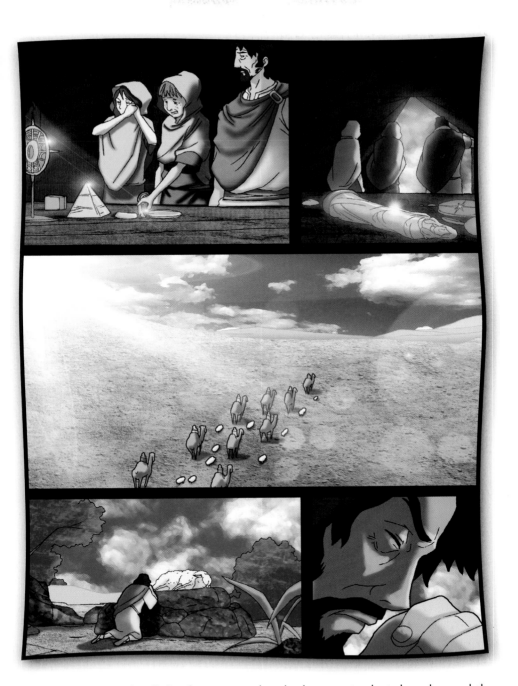

They gave to Jacob all the foreign gods which were in their hands, and the rings which were in their ears. The terror of God was on the cities that were around them, and they didn't pursue the sons of Jacob. So Jacob came to Bethel and Jacob built an altar there. God said to him, "Your name shall not be Jacob any more but Israel." (35:4–35:10)

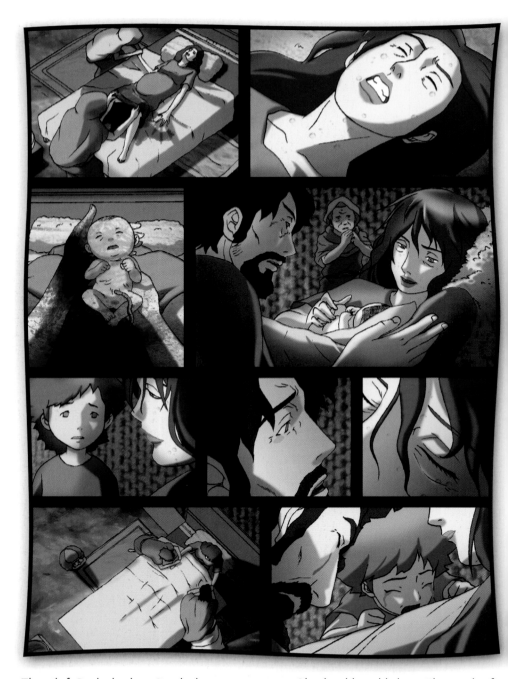

They left Bethel when Rachel was pregnant. She had hard labor. The midwife told her, "Don't be afraid, for you will have another son." It happened, as her soul was departing, that she named him Benoni, but his father named him Benjamin. Rachel died and was buried on the way to Ephrath (Bethlehem). Now the sons of Jacob were twelve. (35:16–35:19)

Joseph, being seventeen years old, was feeding the flock with his brothers in the land of Canaan. Joseph brought an evil report of them to Jacob. Now Israel loved Joseph more than all his children because he was the son of his old age, and he made him a coat of many colors. His brothers saw that their father loved him more, and they hated him. (37:1–37:4)

Joseph had a dream and told it to his brothers, "We were binding sheaves in the field, my sheaf arose and your sheaves bowed down." His brothers hated him all the more for his words. He dreamed yet another dream. He told it to his father and to his brothers. His father rebuked him. His brothers envied him. (37:5–37:11)

His brothers went to feed their father's flock. Israel said to Joseph, "Go see whether it is well with your brothers." Joseph went after his brothers. They saw him and said one to another, "Behold, the dreamer comes. Let's kill him, and we will see what will become of his dreams." (37:12–37:20)

Reuben said to them, "Shed no blood. Throw him into this pit but lay no hand on him." Reuben planned to save Joseph and restore him to his father. When Joseph came, they stripped the coat of many colors, and they threw him into the pit. (37:22–37:24)

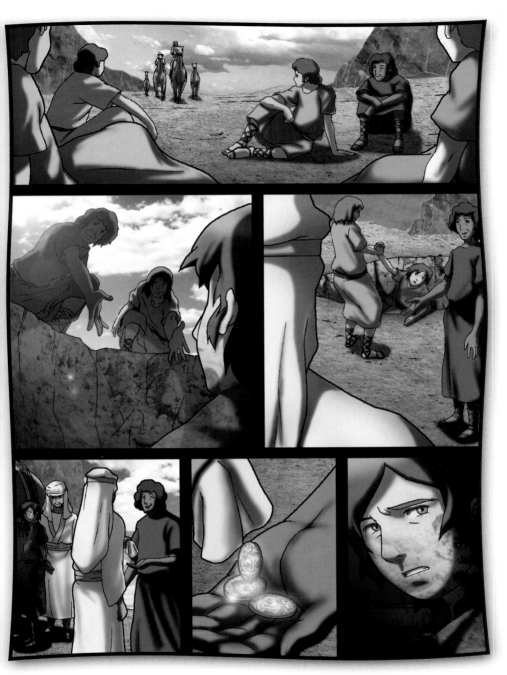

Reuben left as they sat down to eat bread. A caravan of traders on its way down to Egypt approached them. Judah said to his brothers, "Let's sell him and not let our hand be on him, for he is our brother, our flesh." His brothers lifted Joseph out of the pit and sold him for twenty pieces of silver. (37:25–37:28)

103

Reuben returned and saw that Joseph wasn't in the pit, and he tore his clothes. They took Joseph's coat, killed a male goat, and dipped the coat in the blood. They brought it to their father and said, "We have found this." He recognized it and said, "An evil animal has devoured Joseph." Jacob tore his clothes and mourned for his son. (37:29–37:34)

Joseph was brought down to Egypt. Potiphar, Pharaoh's captain of the guard, bought him. Yahweh was with Joseph, and the Egyptian saw that Joseph made all that he touched prosper. He made Joseph overseer over his house, and all that he had. (39:1–39:4)

Yahweh blessed the Egyptian's house for Joseph's sake. Joseph was well-built and handsome. His master's wife cast her eyes on Joseph, and she said, "Lie with me." But he refused, "How can I do this great wickedness and sin against God?" (39:5–39:9)

She kept trying, but Joseph didn't listen to her. One day, he went into the house, and there were no other men inside. She caught him by his garment, saying, "Lie with me!" Joseph left his garment in her hand and ran outside. She called to the men of her house, "He came in to lie with me, and I cried with a loud voice. He left his garment and ran." (39:10–39:15)

When Potiphar heard the words of his wife, his wrath was kindled. Potiphar put Joseph into prison. But Yahweh was with Joseph. The keeper of the prison committed to Joseph's hand all the other prisoners. Whatever they did there, he was responsible for it. (39:19–39:22)

Pharaoh was angry with his chief cupbearer and the chief baker. He put them into the prison where Joseph was. They both had powerful dreams one night. Joseph saw that they were sad. They said to him, "We have dreamed a dream, and there is no one who can interpret it." Joseph said to them, "Please tell it to me." (40:2–40:8)

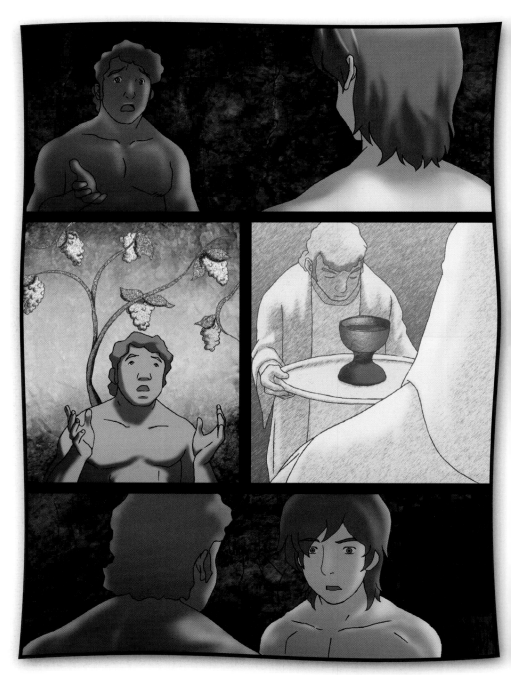

The chief cupbearer told his dream first. "In my dream, a vine was in front of me, and in the vine were three branches. It budded, it blossomed, and its clusters produced ripe grapes. Pharaoh's cup was in my hand, and I took the grapes, and pressed them into Pharaoh's cup, and I gave the cup to Pharaoh." (40:9–40:11)

Joseph said, "The three branches are three days. Within three more days, Pharaoh will lift up your head and restore you to your office. But remember me and make mention of me to Pharaoh and bring me out of this house." (40:12–40:14)

When the chief baker saw that the interpretation was good, he said to Joseph, "In my dream, three baskets of bread were on my head, and the birds ate the bread out of the top basket." Joseph answered, "Within three more days, Pharaoh will hang you, and the birds will eat your flesh." (40:16–40:19)

It happened the third day, which was Pharaoh's birthday, that he made a feast for all his servants, and he lifted up the head of the chief cupbearer, and he restored the chief cupbearer to his position again, but he hanged the chief baker, as Joseph had interpreted to them. Yet, the chief cupbearer didn't remember Joseph. (40:20–40:23)

At the end of two full years, Pharaoh dreamed that seven cattle, sleek and fat, came out of the river and fed on the marsh grass. Seven ugly and thin cattle came up and ate the seven sleek and fat cattle. So Pharaoh awoke, and he called for all of Egypt's magicians and wise men, but there was no one who could interpret his dream. (41:1–41:8)

Then the chief cupbearer spoke to Pharaoh, saying, "I remember a young man, a Hebrew, servant to the captain of the guard, and he interpreted to us our dreams." Joseph was immediately brought from the dungeon. He shaved himself, changed his clothing, and came in to Pharaoh. (41:9 -41:14)

Pharaoh said to Joseph, "I have heard it said that when you hear a dream, you can interpret it." Joseph answered, "It isn't me. God will give Pharaoh an answer." He continued, "Behold, there come seven years of great plenty throughout Egypt. There will arise after them seven years of famine that will consume the land." (41:15 -41:32)

"Let Pharaoh look for a wise man and set him over the land of Egypt. Let them gather all the food of these good years that come and let them keep it. The food will be for a store against the seven years of famine. This way, your people shall not perish in the famine." (41:33–41:35)

Pharaoh said to Joseph, "Because God has shown you this, only I will be greater than you." Pharaoh took off his ring and put it on Joseph's hand, arrayed him in fine robes, put a gold chain about his neck, and set him over all the land of Egypt. Pharaoh gave him Asenath, daughter of Potiphera, priest of On, as a wife. (41:39–41:45)

Joseph was thirty years old when he stood before Pharaoh. During the next seven plenteous years, Joseph laid up grain until he stopped counting. To Joseph were born two sons. Then the seven years of famine began, just as Joseph had said. There was famine in all lands, but in Egypt, there was bread. (41:46–41:54)

Jacob said to his sons, "I have heard that there is grain in Egypt. Go down there and buy some for us so that we may live." Ten brothers went down to buy grain from Egypt, but Jacob didn't send Benjamin. "Lest perhaps harm happen to him." Joseph's brothers came and bowed themselves down to him. (42:1–42:5)

Joseph recognized his brothers, but they didn't recognize him. "You are spies." They answered, "No, my lord, your servants have come to buy food. We are twelve brothers; the youngest is with our father, and one is no more." Joseph said, "Send one of you for your brother to prove you speak the truth or else surely you are spies." He then put them into jail. (42:8–42:17)

Joseph said to them the third day, "Let one of your brothers stay in prison, while the rest go with grain. Bring your youngest brother to me and the one who stays won't die." They spoke to each other in their languuage, "This is because of what we did to Joseph." Reuben answered, "Didn't I tell you? 'Don't sin against the child.'" (42:18–42:22)

They didn't know that Joseph understood them. He turned away from them and wept. Then he took Simeon and bound him before their eyes. Then Joseph gave a command to his servants to fill their bags with grain and to secretly restore each man's money into his sack. (42:23–42:25)

They loaded their donkeys and departed. One of them opened his sack and he saw his money. He said to his brothers, "My money is in my sack!" They turned trembling, saying, "What is this that God has done to us?" They came to Jacob their father and told him all that had happened. (42:25–42:29)

Jacob said to them, "Joseph is no more, Simeon is no more, and you want to take Benjamin away." Reuben spoke to his father, saying, "Kill my two sons, if I don't bring him back to you." Jacob said, "My son shall not go down with you, for his brother is dead, and he only is left." (42:36–42:38)

When they had eaten up all the grain, their father said to them, "Go buy us a little more food." Judah spoke, "The man warned us, saying, 'You shall not see my face unless your brother is with you.'" Israel said, "Why did you tell him that you had another brother?" They said, "We just answered his questions." (43:2–43:7)

Israel said to them, "If it must be so, then do this. Take the choice fruits of the land and a little balm, honey, spice, myrrh, nuts, and almonds and take back the money that was in your sacks. Take your brother, and may God Almighty give you mercy before the man, that he may release to you your other brother and Benjamin." (43:11–43:14)

The men took Benjamin, went down to Egypt, and stood before Joseph. When Joseph saw Benjamin, he said to the steward of his house, "Bring the men into the house, and butcher an animal, for they will dine with me at noon." The man did as Joseph commanded and brought the men to Joseph's house. (43:15–43:17)

They were afraid and said, "Because of the money, he may attack us and seize us as slaves." They said to the steward, "Oh, my lord, we indeed came down the first time to buy food. But when we opened our sacks, each man's money was in the mouth of his sack. We have brought it back, along with other money to buy more food." (43:18–43:22)

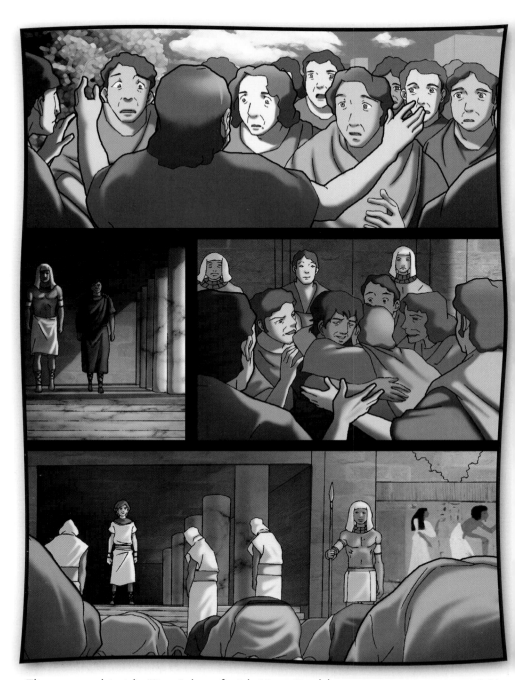

The steward said, "Don't be afraid. Your God has given you treasure." He brought Simeon out to them. The man brought them into Joseph's house, and gave them water and they washed their feet. When Joseph came, they gave him the presents and bowed down. Joseph asked, "The old man of whom you spoke? Is he well?" (43:23–43:27)

They said, "Your servant, our father, is well." They bowed down humbly. Joseph lifted up his eyes and saw Benjamin, his brother, his mother's son, and said, "Is this your youngest brother?" He said, "God be gracious to you, my son." Joseph left the room and wept. He washed his face, and came out, saying, "Serve the meal." (43:28–43:31)

The Egyptians ate at their own table because Egyptians don't eat with Hebrews. Joseph sent food to the brothers' table, but Benjamin's portion was five times as much as any of theirs. They drank and were merry. Joseph told the steward, "Fill their sacks with food and put each man's money back in his sack. Put my silver cup in the sack of the youngest." (43:32–44:2)

As soon as the morning was light, the men were sent away. When they had gone out of the city, Joseph said to his steward, "Follow after the men. When you overtake them, ask them, 'Why have you rewarded evil for good?'" The steward and his guards did as Joseph said. (44:3–44:5)

The brothers said to him, "Why should we steal silver out of your lord's house? With whomever of your servants the cup is found, let him die." The steward said, "Let it be according to your words." The cup was found in Benjamin's sack, and the other brothers tore their clothes as they returned to the city. (44:7–44:13)

The brothers came to Joseph's house and fell on the ground before him.
Joseph said, "Don't you know that such a man as I can indeed divine?"
Judah said, "We are my lord's servants." Joseph said, "The man in whose
hand the cup was found, he will be my servant, the rest of you go in peace
to your father." (44:14–44:17)

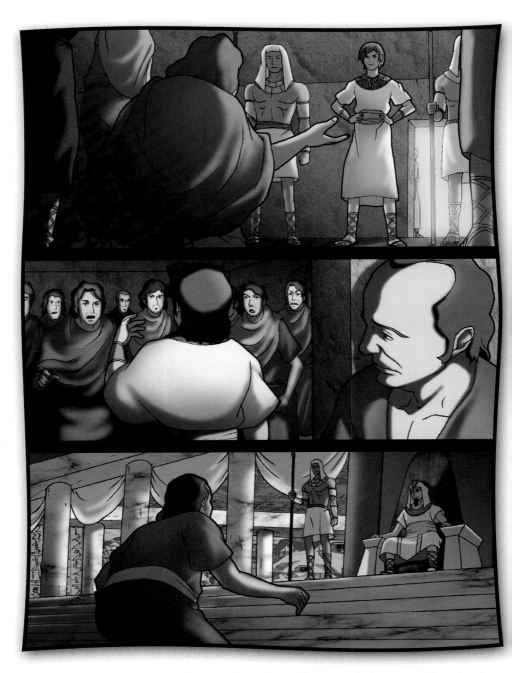

Then Judah came near to him and said, "When our father sees that the boy is no more, he will die. Please let me stay instead of the boy." Then Joseph cried out to the Egyptians, "Everyone leave!" Then he wept aloud as he said to his brothers, "I am Joseph!" But the steward heard what he said. (44:18–45:2)

His brothers were terrified, but Joseph said, "I am Joseph, your brother, whom you sold into Egypt. But don't be afraid. For it wasn't you who sent me here, but God. Hurry, go to my father and tell him, 'God has made me lord of all Egypt. Come down to me now.'" He fell on Benjamin's neck, and wept. He then kissed all his brothers. (45:3–45:15)

Pharaoh, knowing the truth, said to Joseph, "Tell your brothers I will give your family the best land of Egypt." Joseph gave them changes of clothing, but to Benjamin, he gave three hundred pieces of silver and five changes of clothing. As they left he said to them, "See that you don't quarrel on the way." (45:17–45:24)

They went to Jacob, their father. They told him, "Joseph is still alive, and he is ruler over all the land of Egypt." Jacob fainted, for he didn't believe them until he saw the wagons, which Joseph had sent to carry him. Then he said, "Joseph my son is still alive. I will go and see him before I die." (45:25–45:28)

God spoke to Israel in the visions of the night. He said, "Don't be afraid to go down into Egypt, for there I will make of you a great nation. I will also surely bring you up again." Joseph prepared his chariot, and went up to meet Israel. He fell on his neck and wept a good while. Israel said to Joseph, "Now I may die in peace." (46:1–46:30)

Joseph went in and told Pharaoh, "My father and my brothers have come." Pharaoh spoke, "The land of Egypt is before you. Let them dwell in the land of Goshen. If you know any able men among them, then put them in charge of my livestock." Jacob blessed Pharaoh and returned to his father and brothers. (47:1–47:10)

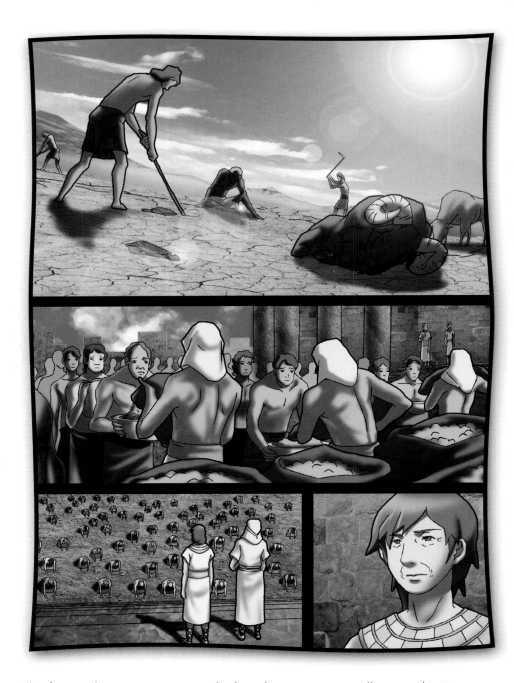

The famine became worse, and when the money was all spent, the Egyptians came to Joseph and said, "Give us bread." Joseph said, "I will give you food for your livestock." Then the Egyptians sold the land, and it became Pharaoh's. Then Joseph said to the people, "Here is seed for you. Sow the land and give a fifth to Pharaoh, and the rest is yours." (47:13–47:24)

The children of Israel lived in the land of Goshen, and they were fruitful and multiplied exceedingly. Jacob called to his sons, "Assemble yourselves. All twelve tribes of Israel. Bury me with my fathers." Jacob yielded up the spirit, and Joseph fell on his father's face, wept, and kissed him. (47:27–50:1)

Pharaoh said, "Go up, and bury your father." Joseph went up to bury Jacob, and with him went up all the servants of Pharaoh, the elders of his house, all the elders of the land of Egypt, all the house of Joseph, his brothers, and his father's house. Only their little ones, their flocks, and their herds, were left in the land of Goshen. (50:4–50:8)

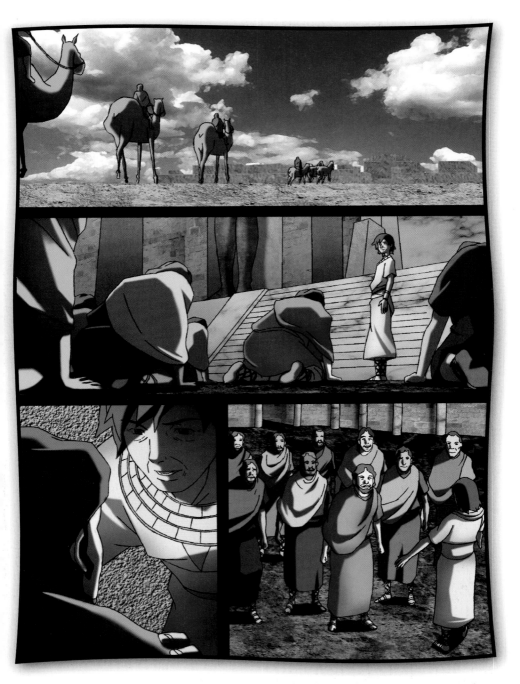

When Joseph's brothers saw that their father was dead, they fell down before Joseph in fear for their lives, and they said, "Behold, we are your servants." Joseph said to them, "God meant it good to save many people. Don't be afraid." He comforted them, and spoke kindly to them. (50:15–50:21)

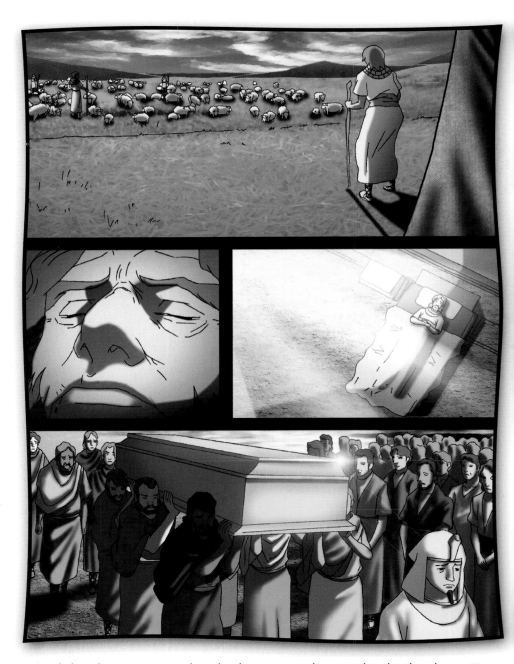

Joseph lived in Egypt one hundred ten years then said to his brothers, "I am dying, but God will surely bring you up out of this land to the land which he swore to Abraham, to Isaac, and to Jacob. You shall carry up my bones from here when that time comes." So Joseph died, being one hundred ten years old, and he was put in a coffin in Egypt. (50:22–50:26)

THE ALMIGHTY BIBLE

GENESIS MAP

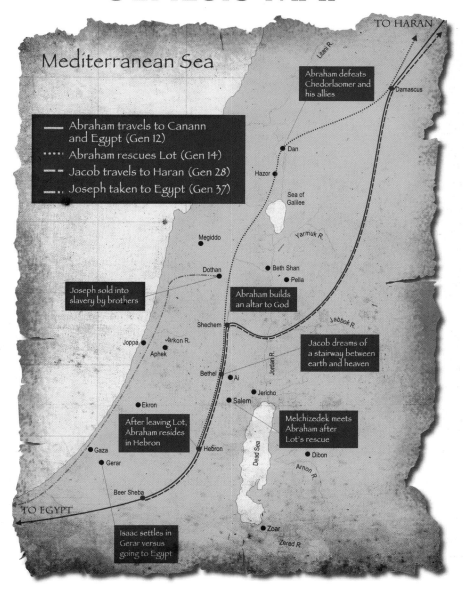

TO HARAN

Mediterranean Sea

Abraham defeats Chedorlaomer and his allies

Damascus

—— Abraham travels to Canann and Egypt (Gen 12)
···· Abraham rescues Lot (Gen 14)
– – Jacob travels to Haran (Gen 28)
–··– Joseph taken to Egypt (Gen 37)

Litani R.

Dan

Hazor

Sea of Galilee

Yarmuk R.

Megiddo

Dothan

Beth Shan

Pella

Joseph sold into slavery by brothers

Abraham builds an altar to God

Shechem

Jabbok R.

Joppa

Yarkon R.

Aphek

Jordan R.

Jacob dreams of a stairway between earth and heaven

Bethel

Ai

Jericho

Ekron

Salem

After leaving Lot, Abraham resides in Hebron

Melchizedek meets Abraham after Lot's rescue

Dead Sea

Gaza

Dibon

Gerar

Hebron

Arnon R.

Beer Sheba

TO EGYPT

Isaac settles in Gerar versus going to Egypt

Zoar

Zered R.